POWER
from the
PODIUM:

The Story of Black Olympians
Tommie Smith and John Carlos

R.A. Ptahsen-Shabazz, Ph.D.

Artwork by
Kephera Ife

where words connect

POWER

from the

PODIUM:

The Story of Black Olympians
Tommie Smith and John Carlos

Power from the Podium:
The Story of Black Olympians Tommie Smith and John Carlos

Copyright © 2024 R.A. Ptahsen-Shabazz, Ph. D.

ISBN: 978-1-959811-72-5 (Hardcover)
ISBN: 978-1-959811-80-0 (Paperback)
ISBN: 978-1-959811-73-2 (eBook)
Library of Congress Control Number: 2024919553

Artwork: Kephera Ife
Book Cover Design: Amit Dey
Interior Design: Amit Dey
Editor: Marjorie Winful
Author Photo Credit: Patrice Samara

Website: www.wordeee.com
Twitter.com/wordeeeupdates
Facebook: facebook.com/wordeee/
e-mail: contact@wordeee.com
Published by Wordeee in the United States, New York, New York 2024

Printed in the USA

ADVANCE PRAISE

"Dr. R.A. Ptahsen-Shabazz, has written a powerful book for wide audiences—from middle school to senior citizens—about the peaceful protest for human rights when Tommie Smith and John Carlos raised their fists at the 1968 Summer Games. The narrative, along with the engaging colorful images, makes it a must read at a time when there are attempts to ban essential books about 20th century Africana and American history."

—Ronald J. Stephens,
Professor of African American Studies,
Purdue University
Author, Robert Franklin Williams Speaks:
A Documentary History

"Power from the Podium: The Story of Black Olympians: Tommie Smith and John Carlos by Dr. R.A. Ptahsen-Shabazz is a powerful and visually compelling tribute to two of the most iconic figures in sports history. Through vivid illustrations and thoughtful narration, Ptahsen-Shabazz captures the courage and conviction of Smith and Carlos, whose Black Power salute at the 1968 Olympics became a symbol of resistance and a call for justice. This book not only celebrates their athletic achievements

but also highlights the enduring impact of their activism, making it an essential read for anyone interested in the intersection of sports and social justice."

—*Nathaniel Norment, Jr., Ph.D.,*
Professor, Director of the Writing Center
The Black Ink Project, and the National Writing Project Site
Professor Emeritus, CCNY and Temple University
Morehouse College, Department of English

"With brilliance and insight, Dr. R.A. Ptahsen-Shabazz has breathed life into the amazing story of Black Olympians, Tommie Smith and John Carlos. In doing so, he provides a guiding light to contemporary readers who seek motivation and empowerment from this great moment in Black history. It is a story that is boldly told and will inspire generations to come."

—*Dr. Annette Teasdell,*
Assistant Professor of Curriculum and Instruction
Clark Atlanta University

"Dr. R.A. Ptahsen-Shabazz's book highlights the raising of a hand covered by a black glove, a jester protesting racial injustice. This simple act against prejudice at the 1968 Olympics in Mexico changed the lives of two African Americans competing for the United States of America. Two of the greatest sprinters ever to wear the red, white and blue stood on the medal podium and showed their disdain for social injustice caused by racial differences. Thank you, Tommie Smith and John Carlos, for daring to be different. Your actions on that day brought on hardships that the public is not aware of. Your courage has affected the lives of so many people not only in America but around the world. You are champions on and off the track. You made a difference, you changed the world; appreciate your efforts as role models and teachers of integrity."

"Dr. Ptahsen-Shabazz has captured the spirit of the Olympic Movement for Human Rights. This book will bring many historical facts into focus, and serve as an introduction to much needed discussion, and sociological workshops, on the relationship between Sport and Society. I was a student-athlete during these critical years (1967-1970) and a close friend of five of the athletes who reached the podium at the 1968 Mexico City Games. His literary style is congruent with the psychological language of the USA Olympians of that Olympiad. His reference to Jesse Owens is a critical piece of the dynamics of that protest. *Power from the Podium* should be a "must read" for Collegiate athletes in coming years."

"*Power from the Podium* offers a reverential account of two important figures in African American activist and sports history. Careful consideration is given to reach an audience of young minds that will benefit from an encounter with the potent nature of Black stories. The elevation of cultural consciousness is an important objective that Dr. R.A. Ptahsen-Shabazz seeks to facilitate with colorful illustrations that provide powerful visuals and words that generate imaginative imagery to leave a lasting impression upon the reader."

"*Power from the Podium* is an incredibly detailed reflection including insightful accounts of the Olympians' successes, struggles and obstacles in front of and behind the camera. I am so grateful for the reminder given by Jessie Owens, "I could have done more." The reality is we all can and should do more. This book will not disappoint!"

—*Christina Anderson,*
Head of School
Westbury Friends School

"Long before football player Colin Kaepernick took a knee to protest the killing of George Floyd, Black Olympians Smith and Carlos became the first athletes to use their sport to advocate for social justice. Dr. Shabazz tells the story of this pivotal moment at the 19th Olympics with the passion and historical accuracy the moment deserves, creating awareness about the plight of Black athletes who stand up for human rights."

—*Professor Marcia L. McNair*
Nassau Community College

"Dr. R. A. Ptahsen-Shabazz was destined to scribe *Power from the Podium: The Story of Black Olympians Tommie Smith and John Carlos!* Deeply rooted in his personal journey as an incredible scholar-athlete indelibly lives the transformative backdrop narratives of Tommie Smith, John Carlos and the 1968 Olympics. In this masterpiece, he skillfully unites his love and passion for track and field with his deep knowledge of Africana/Black scholarship, resulting in an essential read that celebrates Black excellence in the face of the stark realities of oppression. This essential work will inspire young readers to live their visions and stand as beacons of change for their families, communities, and world."

—*Kamau Ptah, Author*
Crossing the Threshold; Embracing the Call
Rites of Passage Specialist,
Educational Consultant & Healing Drum Practitioner

TABLE OF CONTENTS

TRIBUTE AND LIVICATION

For our father, Frank J. Patterson, Jr. (in heaven) and
my brother's Godfather, Charles R. Poussaint;
in remembrance of the days spent at meets and practices,
initiating our lifelong love for track and field,
complementing our eternal love for you both.

FOREWORD

In the late 1960s the entire world was in the midst of political change—from Vietnam to Africa to America. Even days before we got to Mexico, the students had been massacred there by their own military for protesting. The poor, have-nots would no longer remain quiet. Protest was the expression of the era and I was groomed and ripened, with my generation, into a budding manhood that would not be quieted. Our lives would be self-defined and self-articulated, respected or not by the rest of the world.

As a Harlemite, self-respect was always my life's prerequisite. Give us liberty or.... We had months of debating and deliberating over the idea of Professor Harry Edwards' proposed 1968 Olympic Black-out (I like this book's critique of the term "boycott"), where Black athletes would not participate in sport and represent a country that refused to justly acknowledge our equal humanity.

The majority of Black Olympic hopefuls unfortunately decided to reject the Olympic Black-out and participate in the Games. This decision had its Black dissenters, including Lee Evans, Tommie Smith and me. UCLA basketball star, Lew Alcindor (Kareem Abdul-Jabaar), maintained the Black-out and didn't play ball in Mexico at all! Many are called, few are the chosen.

Lee, Tommie and I decided to go to Mexico and make a statement. We were given the athletic talent and discipline by God that would put us in the position to spark a world consciousness regarding justice for Black people and humanity's other poor, despised and rejected. We embraced being "The Chosen" to bring some statement to what was meant to be merely fun and "Games."

As I stated, the late 1960s were a time of change. We were a generation that was changing the world. Our statement on the medal stand was our protest of the time. Our talent put us in a position to make a statement for the movement. I can't say I was thinking of being an historical icon. It was protest for a change that we saw on the verge of manifesting. At that time, in that moment the thought that our statement, power from the podium (this book's title), would be needed for generations to come was not in our youthful minds.

In our early twenties, witnessing and participating in the brave and bold commitment that the brightest and the best of the 1960's generation was waging against the world powers, we truly believed that revolution was eminent in our times. However, in my youth I met Malcolm X and he said in the process of revolution, "You have to wake the people up first to their humanity and to their heritage. Then you'll get action."

I am grateful to be an awakening icon from that time, as Muhammad Ali would say, "For all times!" R.A. Ptahsen-Shabazz's *Power from the Podium: The Story of Black Olympians Tommie Smith and John Carlos*, with its colorful artistic depictions by Kephera Ife, warmly captures the nestling and nurturing of our youthful days.

Although we never ran the hurdles in competition, both of our lives were challenged with many hurdles. This narration of our story, for all ages, helps to show that when we are young, awakened, focused and supported in our talents and commit to the betterment of our society and the world, we all can take the hurdles in stride and ascend to become iconic representatives for justice in our times.

Dr. John Carlos
Olympic Bronze Medalist
1968 Summer Olympics

Chapter One

"ON YOUR MARKS"/LISTEN FOR THE GUN

"*Correras a las marcas* (Runners to your marks)," the Mexican starter commands the sprinters. "*Listos* (Ready)...." **POW!**

The 1968 Olympic men's 200-meter finals begins as the runners come out of their starting blocks and sprint their ways around the track's final turn. The main competitors for the gold medal are Tommie Smith and John Carlos of the United States (U.S.). The month before, both sprinters broke the world record in the 200 meters at the U.S. Olympic Trials at Echo Summit in the Sierra Nevada Mountains of Lake Tahoe, California. Carlos took first place.

In Mexico City's stands, 100,000 Olympic fans from around the world cheer from their seats for their countries' fastest competitors. The excitement of the day makes the fans forget the horrific and tragic events of the previous week. Days before the Olympics began, young college and high school students were shot down by Mexico's military troops while peacefully protesting against the Mexican government. The students were expressing their frustration and contempt for their government's financially careless attitude in spending millions of dollars for the Olympics while the country's masses of people struggled in, or close to, poverty.

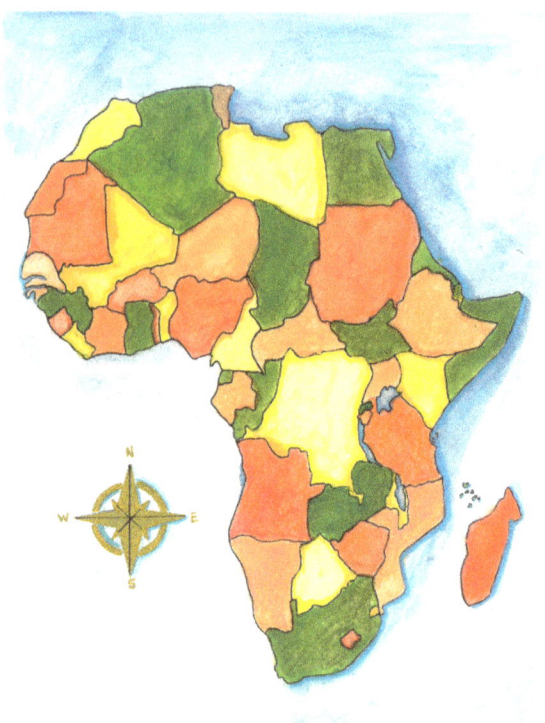

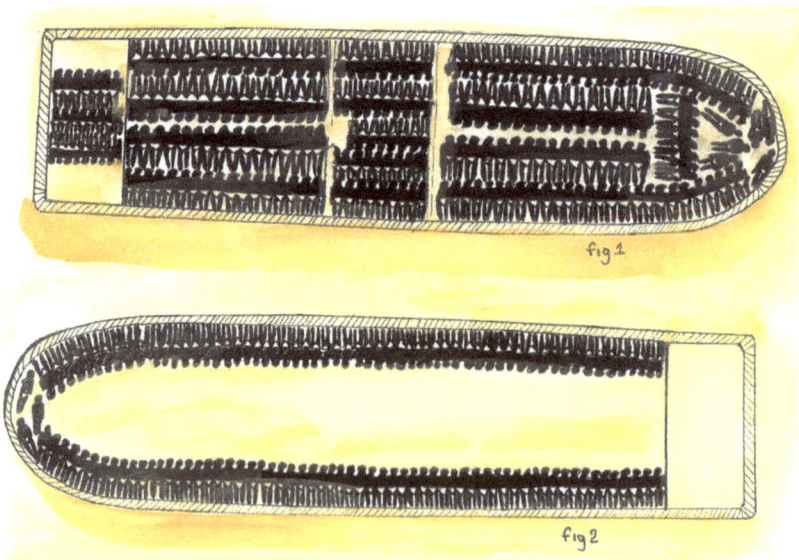

fig 1

fig 2

Although born on opposite sides of the United States, African American Olympians Smith and Carlos could closely relate to the reasons for the Mexican students' protest. The two men were similarly inspired to use their athletic prowess to achieve personal goals as well as arouse the consciousness of a people's movement for human rights. Both men had grown up in poverty, yet because of distinctly different childhoods, they were quite different in attitude. John Carlos was born June 5, 1945 and raised a poor East Coast city slicker in the great and fabled Black community of Harlem in New York City.

Tommie Smith was born June 6, 1944 in Clarksville, Texas. He was raised poor in the fields between Texas and Central Valley, California where he and his large family moved when Tommie was six years old. His family, which grew to eventually reach twelve children, survived on the limited job opportunities that have been available to Blacks in the United States since the ending of slavery.

Over *100 million* Africans were kidnapped from West and Central Africa to be brought to the Western Hemisphere for 300 years in the bellies of European slave ships. Those who survived were tortured and terrorized until arriving, only to be sold and purchased on European auction blocks established for Africans after the Europeans stole and colonized the Western Hemisphere's over 500 nations of Indigenous people that Christopher Columbus mistakenly misnamed "Indians."

As he grew up, all the members of Tommie's family picked and chopped cotton as sharecroppers from "sun-up to sun-down" in sun-blazing Central Valley, California. Sharecropping involved working crops as farmers on land owned often by the White descendants of slave "owners." Tragically, sharecropping was often the only income for African American families attempting to ascend from slavery. However, sharecropping was a new type of slavery, still ruthlessly

exploitative, harsh, and often no less brutal in labor and reprimanding repercussions.

John Carlos, like Tommie Smith, grew up with his parents and siblings. John's father, "Big Earl" Carlos, was the son of a South Carolina sharecropper. Big Earl was a World War I army veteran with his own Harlem store where he served the community as a shoemaker. He and John's Jamaican-born, Cuban-raised mother guided their three sons and one daughter through the perilous concrete jungle that Harlem was decaying into by the 1950s. Young Johnny was coming into double digits in age. His parents had the immediate worry for their children navigating a Harlem that was becoming notoriously known for drug addicts and pushers roaming the streets.

As lack of opportunity defined "country" life on the West Coast for Tommie Smith's family, similar injustices of U.S. society's inequalities plagued John Carlos' family in East Coast "city" life. Both Tommie and John's young lives were filled with problems of poverty. Their families, like millions of African American families, had sadly inherited poverty as a result of never being healed, fairly educated, nor compensated for 300 years of slavery and the on-going 160 years of White racism and discrimination that have followed.

Now, on October 16th, 1968, were Tommie Smith and John Carlos running for Olympic glory in Mexico City! Fate clearly aligned their special destinies from childhood to the famous infamous moment after their race that would greatly define the rest of their lives.

Chapter Two

WORKING HARD FOR THE MONEY

As soon as Tommie's family moved to California from Texas, the only job available for them was in a labor camp! *The whole family* immediately was sent again to the fields and after work, a cold shack would be called home. Working in the labor camp would be how their trip from Texas would be paid off by the landowners who paid their bus fare to California.

Young Johnny grew up with his family in a Harlem government housing project. Although his shoemaker father owned his own neighborhood shop, to make ends meet, like with Tommie's family, everyone in John's family was encouraged to work. Vioris, John's mother, worked the night shift as a nurse's aide in Manhattan's Bellevue Hospital. Johnny and his brothers worked in Big Earl's shop after school.

Sometimes at night Johnny and his friends would go to "hustle" some money at some of Harlem's most legendary night clubs. Half a New York City block from John's house was the star-studded Savoy Ballroom. The legendary Savoy Ballroom was a hot spot of

the neighborhood and what Harlem Renaissance writer Langston Hughes called the "Heartbeat of Harlem." John and his buddies would open cab and limousine doors for cash tips from famous singers and actors attending the club. Stars like Louis Armstrong, Frank Sinatra, Ella Fitzgerald, Lena Horne, Billy Holiday, and Fred Astair were big names and generous tippers. Other fun times were had when, outside the club, his crew would dance to make-shift rhythms while Johnny collected the tips from the Savoy's entering crowds.

Like Tommie's living conditions in California, John's home in the Harlem projects had no crystal stairs. But growing up in Harlem in the 1950's and 60's, young Johnny saw demands for change and justice everywhere. Nationally, Dr. Martin Luther King, Jr. and his Southern Christian Leadership Council (SCLC) organization had a country of Black sympathizers and supporters of his leadership in the Civil Rights movement. In Harlem, John would see similar leadership in the Reverend-Congressman Adam Clayton Powell, Jr. and even have the honor and distinction of walking and talking with Malcolm X. These experiences would strongly influence young John to stand up against racism and injustice.

Inspired by the movements for justice of the time, John responded in high school to the serving of poor cafeteria food by walking into the principal's office and waging the request, on behalf of the students, that, "We need a better quality of food." After ignoring John and pushing him out of the office, John stood before the slammed door, took a deep breath and walked back into the office with the demand, "You have forty-eight hours to take care of it; not a threat, but a money back guarantee. If you don't handle it, I will."

After leading a cafeteria strike for two weeks against a daily menu of nasty, un-plucked chickens served with feathers, John again met the principal, whose careless attitude had not changed. "I told

you nothing is going to change," the principal smirked. To this John replied, "Let's see what the public has to say. I'm going to call *The New York Times*, the *New York Daily News,* the *Amsterdam News,* and other Harlem press and see if they have a story here." Once hearing about these possible repercussions, the principal immediately changed from mean to nice and well-plucked, feather-less chicken became the new standard in the high school cafeteria.

Tommie would also have his share of personal injustices and battles with prejudice growing up in California. In Tommie's first year in California schools his mother, "*Mulla,*" gave him a nickel to buy an ice cream cone after lunch. However, before he could get his first lick, a red-headed White boy knocked the cone out of his hand saying, "Niggers don't eat ice cream." Such experiences would increase Tommie's quiet, bashful, but pensive and perceptive nature.

Tommie's school district in Lemoore, California was integrated with children from the workers in the fields. There were Blacks and Indigenous "Native Americans," like Mexicans and other Hispanics, and there were the local Whites. At school Tommie made friends with children of all colors through his participation in sports. He played many sports including football, basketball and was a center-fielder in baseball.

But in the classroom at Central Union School, Tommie felt the White teachers' favoritism towards the White students. Most teachers made the Black and Brown students feel inferior and bad if they answered a question wrong in class. One teacher, Mr. Focht, was an exception. In the classroom he encouraged *all* the students. And Mr. Focht also happened to be the track coach at Central Union School.

One day at school, Tommie's big seventh grade sister Sally was beating everyone at races outside during gym class. Mr. Focht sent her to get Tommie out of his fourth-grade class for a Central

Union championship dash! He was to race Sally and her classmate Coy, another fast runner at Central. Sally and Tommie used to race in the cotton fields by the swimming hole and he had always eaten her dust.

"On your marks, get set, go!" Coy was a quick starter and beat Sally, but on this day neither Coy nor Sally would have a chance. Tommie's long legs blew them both away in the 50-yard dash across the school's playground lawn. In his history of big races, this could have outranked the Olympics. It would mark the beginning of his career as a sprinter.

The next big challenge for Tommie would be convincing his father to let him race for Central Union. Tommie believed his father approved mainly because Mr. Focht was the coach, and a good, caring man who had quietly assisted the family by helping them find a house and helping his father get a job. Tommie's Daddy thought it was nice that he was faster than Sally, but still expected and needed him working in the fields. Before and after school, at sunup and sundown, Tommie's daily responsibilities involved picking, chopping and watering cotton.

Tommie's daddy had known sports as mostly a dead end for African Americans, no matter how talented an athlete was. In Texas, before moving to California, his father and nine brothers had a baseball team. But the Smith patriarch had come to see the road for his children's success as focused and limited to work, school, and God. *"If you run and you get second place, you'll have to be back in the field with the rest of us next Saturday."* This was Daddy Smith's only requirement as he granted permission. At the time, *it would be the only motivation young Tommie needed.*

Chapter Three

DIVING IN THE DEEP END

The beginning of John Carlos' road to the Olympics would originally focus on his wish to splash his way to victory as a gold medal swimmer. At twelve, Johnny loved swimming and, with little official practice, he won the New York City 200-meter freestyle championship for boys his age. He was ready for serious training when Daddy "Big Earl" was forced to stick a pin in his son's water balloon. "You can't go to the public pool; it's too crowded to practice there. And you can't go to a private pool because they don't let Blacks join the private clubs."

Telling his talented son about the sad realities of northern segregation hurt Big Earl more than his son, although young Johnny was also devastated. His first dream to be an Olympic swimmer was sunk because of racism. It wouldn't be the last time American society would make him feel less than others because of the color of his skin.

Quickly moving on to the next sport for which to have Olympic dreams, Johnny put boxing gloves on to give New York's Golden Gloves a try. But Johnny's mother, a nightshift nurse familiar with head traumas, put another dead end on his young Olympic dream as she knocked boxing out of his ring of choices for sports. With both swimming and boxing out of the picture, the next choice seemed obvious to everyone, even the local police!

As he got older, in addition to protesting for better lunches in school, John had become a real supporter of the poor in Harlem, even as Malcolm X had said, "By any means necessary." Like the legendary Robin Hood, John would manage to keep his full-time working parents from the knowledge of his activity of breaking into and robbing goods from Bronx freight trains to gift the Harlem poor. But two Black Harlem police officers caught wind of the street news and cornered him one day. People were talking about, 'how fast Johnny can run with those boxes!' Instead of arresting and sending him to New York's Juvenile Detention Center, because of his speed, these two empathetic Black cops gave the 15-year-old Johnny the opportunity to train with one of the country's premier track teams at the time: the New York Pioneers Track Club.

With the opportunity to run with such a big-name team, John laughed and at first rejected the idea of joining his sad and scrubby Machine and Metal High School track team. They didn't even have a track! However, like Tommie's first coach, John's high school coach, Mr. Youngerman, was a very nice man. Also, like Tommie, John joined the indoor track team coincidentally while watching the team train at the boardwalk one day. Coach Youngerman, seeing John present, invited him to participate in a 100-yard dash. With street clothes and big heavy clodhopper shoes on, John lined up. Again, like Tommie, John had the fastest runners at his high school eating his dust. Coach Youngerman yelled out, "We got a *phenom* here!"

But as nice a man as Coach Youngerman was, niceness was all he brought to coaching; he unfortunately knew nothing about the sport of track and field. How frustrating this would be for the super competitive ego that had always been part of John's personality. Before their first New York City high school track meet, sweet Coach Youngerman blew the fire out of the team with his own pep

talk. "Guys, just go out there and have fun. You can't beat these guys. Just do your best."

John blew up! "I'm out here to win, and anyone not here to win should get back on the bus!" Coach Youngerman was almost given John's famous "forty-eight hours" speech to get it together. John told his teammates, "Ya'll just get the baton to me close, and we'll be alright."

As the team walked on the scene into the arena from the locker room, the place was electrified like only a New York City track meet from the golden ages could have been with all the legendary teams, from Brooklyn's Boys High to DeWitt Clinton High in the Bronx. No one had heard of Machine and Metal Trade High School when their relay squad took the track. Then John got the baton on the final anchor leg of the 4 x 220 (880 yard) relay and took the team from last to first. Loud cheers erupted from the boisterious crowd. Happily, an invitation to the famous Penn Relays was a sign that John was moving fast in his right lane.

Like John, Tommie's progression in track made him a natural *phenom* as well. Also similar to John, it wasn't track shoes that made Tommie fast. He won his first races in black high top tennis shoes that Mr. Focht gifted him. Sometimes he would run barefoot, and other times he would borrow a teammate's running spikes, though never his actual size. With no shoes, his teammates', or Mr. Focht's shoes, the results were always the same: first place.

By eighth grade Tommie had grown to a tall, lean and strong six feet, three inches, and one hundred, fifty pounds. He towered over the youth his age. The muscles in his lean frame came as a result of working hard his whole life in those fields with his family all year-round. He was always in shape.

High school for Tommie in Lemoore would only be a continuation of his younger years of alienation. White classmates and teachers would further display their anti-Black prejudices and Tommie would continue to withdraw into feelings of being

ashamed of being Black. His main peace of mind would come with his participation in sports. His hope was that it would be his ticket out of Lemoore.

Coach Burton was Lemoore High School's track coach. Like Mr. Focht, Coach Burton was a good man and recognized Tommie's outstanding track and field abilities. In his junior year in high school, without practice in the event, Tommie jumped twenty-four feet, two inches and broke a meet record in the long jump that had belonged to California Olympic decathlon champion, Rafer Johnson. That same junior year in his first 440 ever, Tommie ran the fastest high school time in the nation that year, a blazing 47.7.

Tommie had found the key to open the door to his biggest desire: to get away from Lemoore and those cotton-picking fields! By his senior year in high school, he had received twenty-five letters from colleges interested in giving him a track scholarship based on his junior year performances. He chose San Jose State College (SJSC) in northern California to stay in California, yet be far enough away from Lemoore that he wouldn't have to go back to the fields every weekend. In high school Tommie's father, realizing that education was the only way out of the cotton fields, had begun telling him all the time, "If I had the chance you have, I wouldn't be doing what I'm doing; I'd be doing a lot better." For Tommie they would be big words of inspiration.

Tommie left for San Jose State with the greatest of sadness having to leave his family, planning to never return to Lemoore. He would spend his last summer before he left for San Jose working in Lemoore, in the fields. All these early phases of his life would be so important in his preparation for his famous appearance on the 1968 Olympics medal stand. San Jose State would be the next stage.

Chapter Four

PUMP THE ARMS, LIFT THOSE KNEES

Before eventually attending San Jose State College and achieving his Olympic dream with Tommie, John's road would make some zigzags. When his humble Machine and Metal Trade High School arrived in Philadelphia for the prestigious Penn Relays, once again Coach Youngerman tried to ease the pressure of having to run against the country's best, and in front of 50,000 track fans. His pep talk again encouraged no worries about winning, or even placing. His final words were, "Just get out there and have a good time."

This time it was the 4 x 440, mile relay team that John huddled together, reminding them of his great confidence: "Just stay within fifteen yards and victory is ours." They were excited, but Coach Youngerman may have been right. By the time John got the stick they were in last place, twenty-five yards behind. John had to hit his highest gear on his first stride to begin to make up the distance. Sprinters usually pace themselves over the distance of the 440 yards, quarter mile distance, but by the backstretch John's blazing burst had caught every runner except a skinny White sprinter from Arkansas. The crowd was wild!

However, the beanpole from Arkansas was a smart runner. He held John off around the final turn to the final straightaway when John went into overdrive and blew past him. The 50,000 fans

were roaring! The finish tape was twenty yards away, and then it happened.

In track, the sprinters *disease* of exhaustion is called *riga-mortis*, otherwise known as "the bear." Lactic acid builds in the muscles and the body begins to move in a staggeringly slow motion joined by oxygen debt causing loss of breath and muscle fatigue. A painful reality, *riga-mortis* is accompanied with the sensation as if someone handed you a piano for the last few strides of your quarter mile sprint. John dropped to the track ten yards shy of the finish line grabbing the cinder gravel in his hands, with the greatest pain he had ever experienced. The beanpole strode by to Arkansas' victory. Teammates and coaches ran to the track to see if John was alright.

"The bear caught Carlos; the bear jumped on his back," coaches and runners teased. John was in so much pain that he just laid there thinking this would be his last race. He was ready to quit when he returned to the stands embarrassed, but the crowd mobbed him saying, "That was Olympic speed! If you didn't fall, you would've broken a record!"

Penn Relays was a real wake-up call to his Olympic potential, despite the embarrassing finish line blunder. John now began to practice and have success winning races and receiving positive affirmations. He pursued track and his Olympic dream with the drive and focus he gave to whatever or whoever he loved.

Always in the fast lane, and more and more at odds with his parents as he grew older, John met and quickly fell in love and married a beautiful young girl named Kim that he met at the swimming pool one day with his buddies. Still in high school, young and twisted in emotion and the desire to be his own man and away from his rigidly commanding father, John and Kim were married in Harlem on a cold February day in 1965. While John finished high school impressing college coaches with his race times, Kim worked as a

secretary in Harlem. The newlyweds rented a small apartment across the bridge in the Bronx and in November, Kim gave birth to a baby replica. They named her Kimme.

As John graduated from high school, colleges were interested in him until they saw his grades. Before taking an interest in track, he had not really seen college in his future and didn't put much effort into schoolwork. Now he had hoped to attend San Jose State College and join "Speed City" with Tommie, but his grades were just passing and San Jose State wanted him to attend a junior college first, to get his grades up. With the rejection, John saw his next best option when offered a scholarship by the coach from East Texas State University. However, an introduction to Southern-style segregation would be a trememdous culture shock for a Harlem-born and raised African American.

Arriving with his wife and daughter at the airport in Texas, they were to see in person, as New Yorkers, what they had only seen on television: "White" and "Colored" bathrooms and fountains. "Negros" were called "Nigras," and with the same attitude and tone reflecting the "N" word that they were insinuating. Their unwelcomed arrival would be a sign of difficult days ahead in Texas.

John and East Texas' Coach Brown would have personality conflicts immediately. John was not accustomed to the patronizing expectation of southern Whites, and the acceptance of Blacks, that they should mindlessly follow and not question illogical directions from Whites. Their first conflict would be the day before a track meet when Coach Brown instructed the team to run all of the stadium steps. John firmly insisted it was a bad idea considering it would tire their legs before having to travel the next day, cramped for hours in vans before running in the meet. As John defiantly walked the stairs instead of running them, Coach Brown erupted, picking up a hammer as if to threaten John!

Fortunately, Coach Brown's son was present to restrain his father, but John had seen enough as he marched out of the stadium, quitting, and rejecting the apologies of Coach Brown. John insisted, "I ain't nobody's mule!" It took the begging of all the assistant coaches to get John to return to the team. He always had a nature to be a team player for the collective cause. He would lead the team to become the 1967 Lone Star Conference Track and Field champions.

By the autumn of 1967, the Black human rights movements in America were at a high mark. It wouldn't be long before John's outspoken support of a proposed "boycott" by African American athletes of the 1968 Olympics in Mexico City would bring him at odds with East Texas State. After telling a campus reporter his thoughts in support of the movement, John and all the Black athletes were called to the Athletic Director, Jesse Heathorn's office and ordered not to do anyting that would make East Texas State associated with the "boycott."

John began to feel targeted. It would be the first of times to come when he would feel unsafe for himself and his young family. He had to get out of Texas. At least in New York he would be given cordial respect for his manhood. No one would call him "boy" or "son," or "Nigra!" He had too much Malcolm X, Black man pride to reside in a southern "former" Confederate state. It was the beginning of 1968. John, Kim and Kimme quit Texas and returned to Harlem. In a matter of months, he would come to see that his views as a proud Black man would, in fact, be too much for the whole country.

Fate would have it that the proposed Black "boycott" of the 1968 Olympics was being led by student-athletes at the same San Jose State that John still desired to attend. Tommie Smith, a senior at San Jose State by 1968, was outspoken about the movement along with his teammate, Lee Evans and their guiding professor and 1968 Olympic Boycott organizer, Harry Edwards.

Chapter Five

STRIDE FOR STRIDE

Tommie Smith's transition to San Jose State College was full of intellectual growth and athletic success. Before becoming Silicon Valley and the technology home of millionaires, San Jose was a rural area with the college as its largest attraction. Tommie overcame the intimidation and academic challenge of being among only twenty Black students in the midst of 20,000 mostly White students. Quickly realizing the demands of being a student-athlete, he soon became acquainted with the library and began spending all of his free time there. Tommie spent hours researching, reading, and thinking about the history of America, slavery, the Constitution, and what his role could be to promote awareness to correct such a hypocritical government and country. Although very shy, it would be difficult on campus to hide his six-foot, four-inch height and his 180 pound frame, and to ignore his own pricking sense of responsibility to bring awareness of the racist system.

The prospect of having to return to sharecropping in Lemoore was a strong motivator for Tommie to succeed in college. Choosing a major, Tommie reflected on his family's neo-slavery existence as sharecroppers, and on his new environment at San Jose State where education and tools for progress in life were to be gained by so few Blacks, yet easily accessible to most Whites. To overcome the inequalities of opportunity in America he wanted to comprehend them. He would select Social Science/Sociology as his major and eventually earn his Bachelor's degree from SJSC.

On the track Tommie achieved his greatest success. By the end of his freshman year, he was named Athlete of the Year by the U.S. Track and Field Foundation. The highlight of his season was at the West Coast Relays in Fresno, California. Here Tommie ran the quarter mile (440 yards) blazing stride for stride and nearly beating the defending college champion, losing by a mere lean at the tape to the Army's Dave Tobler. Both were timed at 46.5, at the time the best in the country for 1964.

By Tommie's sophomore year his desire for excellence in track, academics and society began to come together. Under the tutelage of San Jose State's "Speed City" legendary Coach Bud Winter, there were great expectations emerging for Tommie's track career. One spring afternoon in March 1965 Tommie would break two world records in one race!

Coach Winter had set up two finishing lines for the straight-away 200 meters and 220 yards at a San Jose State small triangular meet between the College of the Pacific and University of California, Santa Barbara. The nine-foot measure between 200 meters and 220 yards meant Tommie would cover the distance in one stride breaking both records at the same time with virtually the same time: twenty seconds flat. They would be the first two of eleven world records that Tommie would hold simultaneously, an accomplishment yet to be duplicated.

After the world record performance, Tommie would also set his first mark in social activism. Professor Harry Edwards and other campus leaders organized a protest march in support of the Black

Rights movement in America's south, and the need for racial justice in California as well.

Harry Edwards, himself, was a former Black athlete of San Jose State's basketball and track team as a discus thrower. A towering presence at six feet, eight inches and two hundred-fifty pounds, Edwards had also come from poverty in East St. Louis, Illinois.

Determined to break free of its destitute slums, Edwards used his mind, athletic ability, and size to achieve success. He received his Bachelor's with academic honors at San Jose State, and his Master's at Cornell University returning to San Jose State to teach before going on to the University of California, Berkley to earn his Ph.D. in Sociology.

Immediately after Tommie's world record meet performance, he caught a ride to meet up with the protest marchers who were staying in a gynasium for a night before being en route the next day for a 30 mile walk to San Francisco's City Hall. About 100 student marchers made their way, forced to march through the back streets and off the direct freeway route. Composed of mostly Black students with a sprinkling of Whites, their journey from San Jose to San Francisco was sixty miles altogether.

Inspired by the non-violence spirit of Martin Luther King's activism, the marchers remained peaceful even as local Whites yelled "Niggers" and threw bottles and other objects. It was a frightening reality check of the society's viciousness to Black people for the California college students.

The number of athletes involved in the social protest was impressive. Many served as security on the march, maintaining the peace, order, and discipline. It was a big day for Tommie, for more than the world records. It was his first day merging the success of his athleticism with the social activism and movement for justice of the times. It would only be his beginning.

Chapter Six

MANCOTT: THE OLYMPIC PROJECT FOR HUMAN RIGHTS

1968 Olympics Boycott Major Issue

"Proposal of a few Negro athletes to boycott the 1968 Olympic Games has triggered perhaps the greatest explosion of interest and controversy in the history of track and field.

As of now the boycott remains strictly a proposal, with few takers. But confusion abounds and only two things are certain—there will be a great deal more sound and fury, and the decisions are not yet final."

—*Track & Field News*
December 1967

From American slavery days, psychological chains were used in the form of names given to belittle the self-identities of enslaved African men and women. Although the word *"boycott"* may have a broader historical context than its American usage, in its African American usage the term should be recognized as problematic. When grown women and men protest by refusing to participate in degrading corrupt societal systems, oftentimes

at great personal danger and professional sacrifice, such mature defiance does not represent acts deserving the patronizing moniker "*boy*-cott." The proposed term **mancott** may represent the reality more accurately.

By the time Harry Edwards was a senior at San Jose State he had earned honors as a basketball player and held the national record for the discus in track and field. When he returned to SJSC to teach, for many students including Tommie, Professor Edwards would be their first and only Black professor. His courses were exhilarating. As his student, Tommie began to process White America's commitment to maintain a system that relegates Blacks as ignorant and unequal. Professor Edwards' class sparked Tommie's conscious to question the real status of his American citizenship.

The Olympic Project for Human Rights (OPHR) mushroomed into a national movement based on the local concerns of SJSC Black athletes, which mirrored the social issues and concerns of the masses of Black people. According to OPHR founding member and 400-meter Olympic gold medalist Lee Evans, it was "the fall of 1967 when no one would rent us housing. At that time, the only Black men on campus were athletes. Harry Edwards got wind about our complaints and called a meeting. The Olympic Project for Human Rights came out of us not finding housing."

The emerging group's first act against the overall atmosphere of racism at San Jose State was a proposed Black player *mancott* of the school's opening football game against Texas Western University (today know as University of Texas at El Paso). The threat ultimately brought a cancellation of the football game, improved housing accommodations for the Black athletes, and other allowances to the group's stated demands.

Destiny would seem to be making alignments for the Black athlete to be significant beyond the track and field in the 1968

Olympics. As John returned with his young family to New York City, he received a personal invitation from Professor Harry Edwards to attend an OPHR organizing meeting at the Americano Hotel, across the street from Madison Square Garden on January 17th, 1968. Present to show full support for Professor Edward's vision of the *mancott* was none other than Dr. Martin Luther King, Jr., and Floyd McKissack of Congress for Racial Equality (CORE). Their endorsements showed how meaningful they saw the commitment of the young men and how significant the OPHR's demands were for not only the athletes themselves, but for addressing the corrupt policies infecting American and world institutions.

The official demands of the OPHR were fivefold: 1) the restoration of Muhammad Ali's title, which had been wrongly stripped in June 1967 for his refusal to fight in the U.S. racist war against Vietnam; 2) the removal of notorious White supremacist Avery Brundage as head of the International Olympic Committee (IOC); 3) the disinviting from the Olympics of the two racist apartheid governments, South Africa and Rhodesia; 4) the *mancotting* of the racist New York Athletic Club (NYAC), demanding changes in their discriminating policies; 5) the hiring of more Black Olympic coaches.

In New York City, the OPHR set up an effective *mancott* of an ABC televised Wide World of Sports NYAC track meet. The Student Non-Violent Coordinating Committee (SNCC) Civil Rights group leader H. Rap Brown would join Professor Edwards against the NYAC. The *mancott* would ultimately force the club to end its discriminatory policies, which denied membership to African Americans and Jews but profited from their athleticism in their track meets. Having an international impact, the *mancott* was even supported by the athletes from the then Soviet Union.

Although unable to force the resignation of IOC president Avery Brundage, a renowned racist and anti-Jew, the OPHR joined in the international efforts to successfully halt Brundage's

attempt to reinstate the two disinvited racist apartheid countries of Rhodesia and South Africa. These countries were White
governments that, in their creation, had stolen valuable land in
southern Africa and mistreated the indigenous African people in
some of the most heinous, brutal, and inhumane ways ever witnessed by humanity.

However, it was against the Olympics that the OPHR made
its biggest threat of *mancott* if its demands were not met. In addition to the support of Civil Rights and Black Power activists,
the OPHR also received the support of the top legendary Black
athletes of the era: Jim Brown, Bill Russell, Muhammad Ali,
Lew Alcindor (now known as Kareem Abdul Jabaar), and Jackie
Robinson. The man who would forever be admired for integrat-
ing major league baseball, Robinson would say of the young men
of the OPHR, "I respect their courage…in my day, perhaps we
lacked courage."

Yet, there were some Black *track-letes* that tried to downplay the
racism against Black people in American society and pose a falsely
united U.S. to the world. Their lifelong dreams of Olympic gold
would make them reject the thought of a proposed *mancott* of their
desired Olympic glory. Not many would show the courage and conviction of Lew Alcindor who, indeed, *mancotted* the games entirely.
But to even consider *mancotting*, Tommie and John had to first make
the team.

As John Carlos made his move to SJSC, National Collegiate
Athletic Association (NCAA) rules required him, as a transfer student, to sit out of college competition for one year. Carlos would
not run for SJSC until 1969, after the Olympics. Tommie and John
would never compete together in college. Mexico City would be
their only experience as teammates.

By the conclusion of Tommie's collegiate career, he would fulfill
all of his greatest track aspirations. In 1966, his junior year, he lowered the 220-yard straightaway world record to 19.5 seconds and

reset the 220-yard curve record at 20 seconds flat. In his follow-ing senior year Tommie set the NCAA 220-yard record becoming champion with the time of 20.14. In his last meet at San Jose State, Coach Winter set up a farewell race. Tommie and teammate Lee Evans ran a *smokin'* 400 meters before 5000 fans in the stands, stand-ing on top of cars, sitting in trees, and hanging on fences: standing room only!

Lee Evans heard the gun and bolted in his typical style as if he were running only 100 meters. Tommie ate Lee's dust kicking off of his long spikes as he made his way around San Jose State's cinder dirt track. By the end of the final turn, however, Tommie shifted two gears and began to use his high knee technique and long stride to breeze past Lee and the other runners in the final straightaway to the crowds woos and cheers. Both eclipsed the previous world record, Tommie Smith setting two new marks of 44.5 for 400 meters and 44.8 for 440 yards. The 400-meter mark would last only a year as Lee Evans would obliterate it while winning gold in 43.86 at Mexico City. But before the Olympics Evans, Smith, Carlos, and all U.S. contenders would have to fulfill the requirement to attend Mexico in 1968, which meant having to qualify for the team at the U.S. Olympic trials.

Chapter Seven

OLYMPIC TRIALS *POLITRICKS*

As 1968 came under way, the Olympic Project for Human Rights movement began to gain even more strength. Dr. Martin Luther King, Jr.'s support of the OPHR and his pledge to meet and protest in Mexico City were morale boosters that had given the OPHR movement an aura of legitimacy and a feeling of forthcoming success.

Perhaps it was the Soviet Union's international participation in the *mancott* movement that influenced the International Olympic Committee to withdraw its invitation and not allow South Africa and Rhodesia's participation in the Mexico City Olympics. This capitulation, however, would backfire on the unity of the OPHR *mancott* movement as more athletes waivered away because of the IOC's concessions. Then came the shock felt all over the world.

In the spring of 1968, the OPHR movement and the world was stunned by the April 4,1968 assassination of Dr. King as he stood on a motel balcony in Memphis, Tennessee preparing to go to supper. With the horrific murder of the Prince of Peace, and with the IOC's capitulation in its withdrawal of South Africa and Rhodesia, only the real OPHR stalwarts were still willing to seriously consider

mancotting the Olympics. But no matter what the athletes' perspectives were regarding the *mancott*, they first had to make the U.S. team to even consider the protest.

The track and field student-athlete-activists around Professor Edwards, the central players (runners) truly committed to the OPHR *mancott* were less than a handful: Smith, Evans and Carlos. Their own statements in support of the OPHR made them well known by the track and field world, the IOC's Avery Brundage, and the U.S. Olympic Committee (USOC) as well. These were not the athletes ideally wanted to represent the country. Fearing what they would do if they made the team, the USOC would alter the traditional methods of team selection and hope that Evans', Smith's and Carlos' chances would be impeded.

First would be the need for two trials to select the team. At the first trial in the Los Angeles Coliseum, Tommie and an injured John were among the fastest qualifiers in the 200 meters. Yet, to compete in the finals they would be given the worst lanes: the cramped lane one for John, and the blind lane eight for Tommie. The bias in their lane selection was obvious to all track aficionados. Also obvious was the threat of the Black athlete *mancott* that was made clear by protest placards held up by supporters in the stadium that read: "Why Run in Mexico and Crawl At Home?" Despite the high drama, Tommie, John and Lee all qualified for the second trials held in the high altitude of Lake Tahoe, California.

The USOC said the Lake Tahoe training camp and trials were necessary to prepare for the high altitude of Mexico City. The USOC officials would also use the seclusion of the Echo Summit, Lake Tahoe Olympic training site to threaten the Black athletes. They were told that anyone who embarrassed the U.S. or even mentioned "boycott" would be kicked off the team and not be allowed to compete in Mexico. However, Lake Tahoe was not in the organizing schedule for the OPHR.

Still, irregularities continued on the track for Smith and Carlos. John had recovered from the bad leg with which he ran in Los Angeles where he only qualified in the 200 meters and did not compete in the 100 meters. After recovering from the injury, he had run the fastest 100 meter time in the world coming into Lake Tahoe with a 10.0. However, officials refused to allow him to compete because he had not run the 100 meters in Los Angeles. An incensed protest brought no change for John. Already aware of his outspoken support of the OPHR, they would not want him competing for the Olympic consideration as the world's fastest man.

This meant that it would only be the 200 meters at Lake Tahoe for John, and Tommie too. This race would also bring drama. For Tommie it would now be the challenge of moving his tall frame and 12-foot stride around the narrowest of turns in lane one, "randomly" assigned to him. At the Los Angeles trials he had to win from the other disadvantaged lane: the blind lane eight where one can see no competitors until coming off the turn and unto the final straightaway.

From lane one at Echo Summit in Lake Tahoe, Tommie would trail John who was in top form and, typical to his style, got out the blocks from lane three and blazed the turn. John's world record form and time of 19.7 may have been difficult for Tommie to overcome from any lane that day. John's time smashed Tommie's world record of 20.0, except for another issue of controversy.

John's world record time would be rejected because he was wearing a new Puma style of brush spike shoes that were not approved by the International Association of Athletics Federation (IAAF). Many, including John, felt he had been caught up this time in commercial politics as Adidas, Puma's rival company, had won the contract to sponsor the Mexico City Olympics. Lee

Evans also had a 44.0 seconds world record in the 400-meter nullified at Echo Summit for wearing the same Puma brush spikes. Nevertheless John, Tommie and Lee made the team, but what would it mean?

The final decision over the *mancott* would be deliberated after Lake Tahoe's trials at a meeting in Denver, Colorado moderated by the 1964 Olympics long jump champion, Ralph Boston. Tommie, John, and Lee were present as the Black athletes reviewed the OPHR movement over the 1967-68 time period. It was collectively determined that there would be no official "boycott." This was decided because the meeting revealed how undecided many were. All feared the potential financial consequences of not getting a job after protesting internationally against the U.S. Some athletes were affiliated with the military and feared being charged for treason. Tommie (who cared more for the protest than his participation in ROTC), John and Lee's commitment to *mancott* had them by themselves on an island. The three athletes and Professor Harry Edwards had been the core spokesmen for the *mancott*. Sadly absent in the organization were the voices of women athletes. Despite the failure of an invitation for them to participate, Black women would make their support bold and clear in Mexico.

Chapter Eight

MEXICO CITY: MOMENTS OF TRUTH

Ten days before the opening of the Games of the XIX (19th) Olympiad, Mexico City university and high school students had been in months of continued peaceful protests and rallies against the *downpressive* authoritarian government regime of then president, Gustavo Diaz Ordaz. His Mexican government had invested $150 million ($1 billion in today's terms) in preparation for the Olympics.

Thousands of students had assembled peacefully for months, listening to speeches in protest of their government's neglect of massive poverty and other socio-economic concerns that were showing no signs toward improving, nor redress in the midst of grand Olympic spending and an economic oil boom.

On October 2, 1968 the large gathering of 10,000 peaceful marchers were met at the Plaza of the Three Cultures by 5,000 military troops. Military snipers in surrounding buildings indiscriminately opened fire on the unarmed students, children, supportive bystanders, and even their own military comrades in the mass. The tragedy has come to be known as the Tlatelolco Massacre. When the smoke cleared and the pandemonium settled, there were arguably over three hundred and fifty killed, over one thousand injured and over one thousand arrested. In 2003 U.S. government records

revealed its own role in providing "intelligence reports," riot control training, military radios, weapons and ammunition. In other words, the U.S. set up the military training and character for the mission of the Tlatelolco Massacre.

Ten days after the massacre, as the Olympics began, shamefully not a mention of the bloodshed and carnage by the Mexican government was expressed. The bloodstained grounds at Tlatelolco Square would be whitewashed clean for the Olympic opening ceremonies, and 50 years later families of the young, sacrificed victims have yet to receive any measure of justice for their government's atrocities against its own civilians.

Before and after the massacre, as Tommie Smith, John Carlos and Lee Evans prepared to depart for Mexico City, death threats bombarded their lives by mail and phone calls. Of the core OPHR athletes, no doubt Tommie Smith was most targeted because of an article focused on him in March 1968. In the *Sports Illustrated* article he stated, "I would give up my right arm to win a gold medal in the Olympics, but I wouldn't give up my personal dignity."

Harry Edwards was also a recipient of the death threats. To the disappointment of Smith, Evans, and Carlos, Edwards decided not to travel to Mexico City in their support. Although he had spearheaded the movement from the beginning, the athletes who would make a protest in Mexico City would be acting totally own their own. For them, mental pressures and anxieties were about more than just their races. In Mexico City they would never relax and feel safe.

The threat of an assassin taking aim on their lives on the track or in the streets was real, especially in the atrocious climate of the 1960s. Medgar Evers, President John F. Kennedy, Malcolm X, Martin Luther King, Jr., presidential candidate and Senator Bobby Kennedy, the thousands of murdered African Americans and others to lose their lives battling White segregation and *downpression* (or simply just trying to live), the U.S. atrocities in

Vietnam, and the most recent hundreds slaughtered in Tlatelolco Square were all clear indicators of the dangerously turbulent atmosphere of the era.

As the competition for their 200-meter event began, Tommie and John talked about their disappointment in the failure of the *mancott*. Like two brother-warriors going into battle, they boosted one another in their collective commitment to win medals for an opportunity to make a statement.

Both men easily qualified through the rounds to get to the finals, though Tommie had seemed to suffer a groin cramp in his semi-final victory. The great moment of truth had arrived on the evening of October 16, 1968.

As the starter's pistol fired, John got out of the starting blocks as fast as a bullet in lane four. When he rounded the turn for the final straightaway he had a five meter lead on the competition. Then, one of the most bizarre Olympic track moments took place. At 140 meters John began committing sprinter error number one: he seemingly lost all focus and composure and began looking to his left, in lane three, for Tommie.

It hardly took a glance for Tommie to capitalize on the blunder, accept the invitation and zip past John to pass him for victory. Tommie won the gold medal in world record pace, setting the new 200-meter mark at 19.83. As he leaned for the finish line, a bewildered looking John now looked to his right, in lane six, only to this time invite Australian sprinter Peter Norman to sneak up and nip him at a tape lean for the silver medal. John would reside with third place.

Track and field, like other sports, has its own fair share of mind games. John has said that all he had on his mind was being on the awards stand to make a statement, and he fulfilled that wish with the bronze medal. Tommie and John had established themselves among the fastest men in the history of the world.

THE NEXT MIND GAME WOULD ESTABLISH TOMMIE AND JOHN
AMONG THE STRONGEST MEN OF WORLD HISTORY

Chapter Nine

BLACK STAND AND SALUTE

With the race completed, Tommie and John had fulfilled the first part of their Mexico City mission. The gold medal was, of course, very meaningful to Tommie. Like John, he felt it should be won by someone who really believed in the OPHR mission. And for John too, his stated goal was just to make the award stand, for it was the only place left for them to make a statement to represent the OPHR platform. But what would that statement be?

The awards ceremony for the 200 meters was only 30 minutes after they had completed the final. Although both men had anticipated the moment, their planning for the awards ceremony protest was quite spontaneous, though thoughtful. Most of the Black track and field athletes wore black socks in Mexico City to protest Black poverty in America. But the rest of Tommie and John's most memorable Olympic moment was planned right after the race.

According to John, he put on an African bead necklace to protest Black lynching, and unzipped his warm-up jacket showing a black shirt covering the U.S. jersey to represent the common working man. Tommie wrapped a black scarf around his neck to symbolize Black pride. His former wife, Denise, had purchased the famous (then infamous) black leather gloves when she bought the black socks. Tommie gave the left glove to John as they decided that they would march military style to the awards podium, with their shoes off bearing the black socks to dramatize African American poverty.

Before the two would make their way to their fateful moment, Australian Peter Norman, the second-place silver medalist, inquired about their planning and the OPHR button Smith and Carlos were wearing on their warm-up jackets. John explained to his friendly rival that the buttons represented a protest for human rights. Coming from an equally racist White settler Australian society, Peter said he stood for equal rights. As Salvation Army workers, his family had ostensibly served Australia's dispossessed Black Aboriginal poor. John found a button for him to wear on the podium. The simple supportive gesture would cost Peter Norman his future Olympic career in Australia, as it would for Tommie Smith and John Carlos in the U.S.

Standing on the podium, all three medalists received their awards with polite applause from the Mexico City attendees. As the flags were raised and the first notes of the U.S. national anthem were played in honor of gold medal winner Tommie Smith, the next moment of truth had come.

Tommie's right fist bolted to the heavens from the top centered podium simultaneously with John's left fist (John standing behind him on the third-place podium). They both lowered their heads in a uniquely mournful salute to the flags as Peter Norman stood before them on the second-place stand, oblivious to the gestures of the two men to his rear. For the over one-minute duration of the anthem they held this position. Whether viewed positively or negatively, the non-conforming pose was jolting and captivating to all who witnessed it.

After being shocked into silence during the anthem, detractors of Smith and Carlos booed and whistled against them as they exited the infield across the track going into the stadium's tunnel. To this, the warrior-filled spirits of Smith and Carlos threw up their fists once more in Black pride and defiant rejection of the heckling.

ABC Sports announcer Howard Cosell began the media interrogation, which Tommie handled with poise while explaining the symbolism of their protest and its meaning for African Americans. Tommie told Cosell, plainly:

> The right glove...signified the power within Black America; the left glove my teammate John Carlos wore on his left hand signified Black unity...I thought I could represent my people by letting them know I'm proud to be a Black man.

In the spirit of Muhammad Ali's refusal to serve America in its racist war against Vietnam, Tommie and John would seem to up the stakes in the Black athlete's rejection of a second-class African American citizenship.

THE PAST AS PRELUDE

Jesse Owens, the African American legend who single-handedly debunked German Nazi premier Adolph Hitler's Aryan/White supremacy philosophy and propaganda by winning four gold medals at the 1936 Munich Olympics, was now hired by the USOC to tone down the ideas of protest from the Black athletes. But Owens was standing with the wrong agents of history. Now in his older years, perhaps Owens was progressing in amnesia regarding the abuse he had received from the American Olympic Committee in his own time.

After the 1936 Olympics, Owens' amateur license was stripped after he got homesick and returned to the U.S., suspended by Avery Brundage, then head of the American Athletic Union (AAU). Brundage had set up a European tour of lucrative track meets for the *unpaid* Olympian "amateur" athletes to further financially exploited them after the Berlin Olympic Games. When Owens had had enough, he was summarily suspended, his amateur license revoked. Jesse seemed to forget his own words of protest thirty-two years prior: "This suspension is very unfair to me...This track business is becoming one of the biggest rackets in the world. It doesn't mean a darned thing to us athletes."

Fast forward to 1968: the great Jesse Owens, who had won so much pride for African Americans in the minefield of White supremacy, was now shamefully the representative of the USOC's attempt to silence the athletes. Before the games began, all of the U.S. team met to hear Owens relive his 1936 glories and speak patriotically of his proudest moments standing for the national anthem because it represented freedom. He evoked the idea that representing the U.S. at the Olympics was the greatest thing one could do.

Yet, rebuked after the 1936 Olympics, Owens returned to the U.S. with four gold medals and a Black man's second-class citizenship. A hero with no country, he was unable to eat in restaurants

where he was being honored, unable to hold certain employment, and ultimately reduced to literally racing against horses to earn a pittance of money to support his family. Despite his own history of abuse by the U.S., Owens would still give himself to be exploited at the Mexico Olympiad.

After Smith and Carlos made their medal ceremony protest Jesse came to meet with the U.S. team again. Owens, obviously sent as an agent by his USOC paymasters, chastised Smith and Carlos for their protest and sought information on any other plans of protest. Jesse cried as if his legacy had opened the doors of justice for African Americans and it was now being tarnished. Despite Jesse's disdainful request for the White athletes to leave the meeting, the Harvard U.S. rowing team and hammer thrower, Harold Connolly remained the only White athletes present. John Carlos says that, years after the 1968 Olympics, he spoke with Jesse Owens who regrettably stated, "If I had done more in 1936, we wouldn't have needed a 1968."

Smith and Carlos would be expelled by the IOC from the Olympics, and the IOC pressured the USOC to revoke their visas. They were given forty-eight hours to leave Mexico City for their protest. The Harvard U.S. Olympic rowing team was even threatened with expulsion for their support of Tommie, John and the OPHR. With the immediate consequences given to Smith and Carlos and the open threats from the USOC for supporting Smith and Carlos, the social-political pressures mounted even further on any politically conscious athletes still left to compete.

As Smith and Carlos were preparing to make their way to face the music in the U.S. all eyes now fell on 400-meter favorite and the last major spokesman for the OPHR, Lee Evans. October 18, 1968, the day prior to Tommie and John being expelled from Mexico City, was a day of great pressure for Evans. Coming into the 400-meter final, Evans had set world records in both of the

U.S. trials. The last one, however, was revoked over the same Puma spikes that cost Carlos the 200-meter world record at Echo Summit, California.

Larry James, lined up in lane two for the Olympic final, had barely lost to Evans in both trials by one-tenth of a second in both races. James had been given the world record from Echo Summit because of Evans' unsanctioned Puma brush spikes. Regardless of the shoes, there would be no denying the 400 meter dash of Lee Evans in Mexico City. Most 400-meter runners strategize the use of their energy in intervals to survive over the long sprint distance. The race is known as the most painful of all the sprints.

But for Evans, he alone would know his strategy. To spectators, his 400 meters always strikingly appeared as an all-out sprint of reckless strategy and abandoning energy, with an overpowering overdrive in its last 100 meters. This typical Evans scene would result in Olympic victory, again in a one-tenth of a second lean at the tape to defeat Larry James. Evans' new world record of 43.86 would stand for twenty years.

Evans, James and Ron Freeman would fulfill an African American 400 meter sweep with gold, silver and bronze, but now the world's attention at the victory stand focused not on applauding the victors of the fastest 400 meters ever competed in world history. The focus was on what, if any, would be their protest. A most difficult position the medalists would immediately have to navigate.

What kind of statement should they make? What statement could be more profound than Smith and Carlos'? Did they want to be copycats, make the same statement and get the same consequence? If they made no statement, how would Black America view them? This predicament offered no solution for unanimous victory.

Evans, James, and Freeman mounted their victory podium with waving fists, wearing the Black Power styled black berets popularized by the Black Panther Party, Evans with his OPHR button as well. But the militant apparel did not match the victors' joyful, jubilant, happy aura. Nor did their respectful removal of their berets for the playing of the national anthem satisfy Black America, now thirsty for more unadulterated statements of Black power and militancy. Lee Evans well characterizes the valley of decision in which Smith and Carlos placed the subsequent victors: "How come I didn't do what Tommy and John did? I had to tell guys, 'If you wanted to get kicked off the team you should have made the team and did it yourself.' So, it wasn't easy for me."

With the notable exception of sports broadcaster Howard Cosell's strong editorial support, the Western media illustrated little desire to comprehend the meaning of Smith and Carlos', nor any other Black protest. The famous broadcaster Brent Musburger *infamously* referred to Smith and Carlos as "Black storm troopers," and their protest, a "juvenile gesture."

Nineteen-year-old George Foreman would quickly become the American media darling, not only by winning the heavyweight gold medal in boxing. His biggest and most important accomplishment for them was his obedient patriotic waving of the American flag as commanded by his boxing coach Pappy Gault, another Black man of the Jesse Owens mindset. The American media attempted to use Foreman's genuflecting posture with the flag as its amazing grace for the raw truth of the genocidal racism that the Smith and Carlos protest had revealed for the world to consider when reflecting on Blacks in American society.

As mentioned, Smith, Carlos, Evans and the OPHR would receive subtle teammate support from the black socks or barefoot protests, and even outright statements of colleagues. Vince Matthews, the 1972 Olympic 400 meter gold medalist and member of the 1968 world record setting 1600 meter relay team, welcomed

Tommie and John on their return to the Olympic Village with a sign that read, "We Support Smith and Carlos."

Wyomia Tyus, the first woman to successfully defend her Olympic 100 meter title in 1964 and 1968, gave strong support to Smith and Carlos. Despite the OPHR's admitted oversight and failure to invite Black women athletes as participants for the movement, Wyomia Tyus would still feel great pride in the movement's posture in general, and Smith and Carlos' medal stand protest in particular. After she anchored the women's 400-meter relay to victory, Tyus announced that the relay squad was dedicating their victory to Smith and Carlos and that they were in support of their teammates' protest for human rights. Like Lee Evans, Tyus would also recognize Smith and Carlos as an impossible podium act to follow stating, "Once Smith and Carlos did what they did...I don't think anybody else that had to go to that victory stand could do anything because it spoke volumes for everything and not just for the Olympics, but for the world."

Chapter Ten

AFTERMATH:
THE RACE IS NOT WON BY THE SWIFT, BUT THOSE WHO ENDURE TO THE END

As it would turn out, Tommie and John would be the only athletes expelled from Mexico City for their protest. However, John in humble truth has recognized that it was the students of the Tlatelolco Massacre who suffered the greatest consequences for protests regarding the 1968 Olympics. Although Smith and Carlos suffered greatly from America's social and economic responses to their protest when they returned, John recognizes those students ambushed by their own Mexican military as the "true Olympic martyrs."

While most African Americans felt great pride in the statement Smith and Carlos had made on the awards stand, aside from a "Welcome Home" sign from John's California neighbors, when they returned to the U.S., they received no major hero welcomes. No fans met them at the airport. There was no security, no protection; their only reception was from an aggressive, patronizing U.S. media that had characterized them as un-American. Upon his return, Tommie would be asked to, and leave the ROTC with an honorable discharge.

The spirit of unity and pledges of support from Professor Harry Edwards faded once they arrived in Mexico City, and their relations became virtually non-existent on their return. From before leaving for Mexico, when the OPHR was nationally marketing its grievances with the strong *mancott* threat, Smith, Lee and Carlos were still only college students.

The death threats that the young men, including Edwards, were receiving from the mere planning stages were indicative of the challenges of survival they would face on their return to America from the Olympics, at least for Smith and Carlos. It was known that they would have difficulties with employment. Even before the Olympics, when his *mancott* affiliation became known, Tommie lost his San Jose job washing cars at a car dealer where he was asked to shake customer's hands as *their* world record holder employee.

Smith and Carlos say that Harry Edwards, Jim Brown and others withdrew on their commitments to provide financial support for the survival of their young families on their return from Mexico City. Harry Edwards has insisted that as men we have "to captain our own ships." Yet the challenges the two young men faced were real: hungry wives and children, no steady jobs, no rent money. The two Olympic medalists took nearly any job they could find for money to support their families, and Carlos says he even had to beg and borrow to survive. Besides Lee Evans giving Tommie a place to stay, ironically of all the Black athletes to give assistance, none other than George Foreman would come to the rescue in Carlos' case. John remembers, "With no fanfare…George reached out with some dollars at a financial low point for the Carlos family. But other than Big George, it just didn't happen."

The pressures on Smith and Carlos' families from the American society were more than just financial. The psychological taunting became haunting. Tommie, John and their family members would all be harassed by a barrage of threatening hate mail and more. The pressure would even bring the loss of life!

In 1970, the emotional strain would bring Tommie's mother, *Mulla*, to depart to the Ancestral realm from a brain embolism at only fifty-seven years of age. According to Tommie, "The way she and the rest of my family in Lemoore were treated after Mexico City contributed to my mother's death. They had cow manure, dead bugs, nasty notes, all sorts of junk put in their mailboxes." Sadly, Smith's family would not be the only to suffer the ultimate as a consequence of the Mexico City Olympic power of Smith and Carlos from the podium.

Chapter Eleven

READY...SET...HIKE?

In final acts of desperation to make a living to support their families, both John and Tommie tried to transition their track speed into playing with the National Football League (NFL). Bob Hayes, the former 100 meter world record holder and 1964 Olympic champion, was making a successful career catching passes as a wide receiver with the Dallas Cowboys. The one big difference between Smith, Carlos and Hayes was that Hayes was recruited and played football at the Historically Black College/University (HBCU), Florida Agriculture and Mechanical University (FAMU) in Tallahassee, Florida. Smith had not played football since high school. Carlos had never played the game and had little familiarity with it.

Nevertheless, Tommie would get a small break when former San Jose State football coach Bill Walsh offered him a tryout with the Cincinnati Bengals where he was coaching as an assistant. Coach Walsh would later lead the transition of the San Francisco 49ers into a football dynasty. In Cincinnati, Tommie was only able to make the practice-scout team, paying a mere $1,200 a month. For the weeks he was put on the active roster he would make $900. Compared to the other players making $1,500 and more *a week*, Tommie's $300 a week salary was at the meager bottom.

(Advance for PMs of Tuesday, July 15)
(CE2) WILMINGTON, Ohio, Jun 15--SPRINT CHAMP TO TRY FOOTBALL

Altogether, Smith would play seven games in two and a half years before being cut. Coach Walsh arranged for Tommie to try out in the Canadian Football League (CFL) with the Hamilton Tiger-Cats. After a few months, he was sent home with $2,000. His football career was done. Sadly, John Carlos would have similar football disappointments.

After returning from Mexico City, John's only short-lived peace of mind would be found while continuing his college track eligibility with San Jose State. In 1969, with Tommie's track eligibility at SJSC complete, Carlos and Evans would lead the school to its only NCAA track team championship. Carlos would tie the 100-yard world record at 9.1, and rank number one in the 100 and 200 meters in *Track and Field News'* World Rankings for 1969 and 1970. But track was still an amateur sport, meaning there was no money to make for world records and rankings. Like Tommie, John had mouths to feed. The year 1970 would be his last track season. Like Tommie, he would give the NFL a try.

But unlike Tommie, John had no football experience. Although he was able to sign a contract with the Philadelphia Eagles through a Jim Brown associate, Irv Cross, Carlos did not even know how to put his pads on! And like Tommie, John's NFL career would be short-lived, but not without injury. He would tear ligaments in his knee that were never properly repaired.

Somehow upon being cut by Philadelphia, again like Tommie, an opportunity would arise in Canada with the CFL. This was a great fortune for John. He would negotiate Canadian citizenship for himself and his family as part of his deal with the Montreal Alouettes. Here he would bring his family. John and Kim's children, Kimme and her young brother Malik, would benefit from nationalized healthcare among other perks of Canadian life. But again, like Tommie, John's poor catching "hands of stone" and his injured leg made his CFL career a stint as quick as a sprint.

83

Unable to find sufficient work to care for his family in Canada, John was given an opportunity to do promotional work for Puma at the 1972 Munich Olympics, of all places. This deal included moving his family back to California at his wife Kim's insistence. They would separate as the years of strain had their ultimate impact on the happiness of their union. Tommie's first marriage to his wife, Denise, would also come to an end after his unsuccessful football stint and the excessive unemployment pressures, combined with the psychological strain of persistent death threats and constant Federal Bureau of Investigation (FBI) surveillance.

The air of conspiracy would follow Smith and Carlos throughout the 1970s. With the tragic slaying of the Israelian wrestling team at the Munich Olympics, it turned out that the Palestinian assassins were outfitted in Puma gear, ostensibly received from John's promotional table.

Then there was the 1972 Munich awards stand controversy, which would draw innuendos to Carlos and Smith. Vincent Matthews, from New York, and Wayne Collette from California won gold and silver in the 400 meters. Minutes later, they nonchalantly stood on top of the medal stand ignoring the raising of the flags and the playing of the national anthem, Matthews twirling his gold medal on his index finger as he walked off the awards podium to boos and whistles. Like Smith and Carlos, they expressed feelings of national alienation: being born in a country, but not feeling like full citizens. Unlike Smith and Carlos, Matthews and Collette did not even consider their time on the award stand a protest.

Matthews was present in Mexico in 1968 as a member of the world record breaking Olympic 1,600 meter championship relay team. Wayne Collette would explain to Howard Cosell:

I didn't stand at attention on the victory stand because I couldn't do it with a clear conscience.... My actions on the victory stand probably mirrored the attitude of White America toward Blacks: totally casual, ignoring them...it wasn't a protest...the national anthem went and...I cannot go along with the words because I don't believe that they're true; I wish they were. I think we have the potential to have a beautiful country but I don't think that we do. I guess my statement now will label me as a militant, though really I'm not. But that's how I feel.

For the vulnerable honesty of their Black perspective, Matthews and Collette, like Smith and Carlos before them, would be expelled from the Olympic village and barred for life by the IOC.

The truth regarding the lyrics in the national anthem would come under scrutiny with the 21st century protest of San Francisco 49ers quarterback Colin Kaepernick. Kaepernick refused to stand at attention and, before popularizing the anthem-kneel, he originally sat for the national anthem before NFL football games in light of the unaccountability of the U.S. criminal system in the police killing of unarmed Black people. "There are bodies in the street," declared Kaepernick, "and people getting paid leave and getting away with murder."

Kaepernick's protest would also bring historical consciousness to the social message and cultural meaning of the U.S. national anthem. Why any African "American" would stand for the national anthem is beyond question, considering that Francis Scott Key's anthem celebrates the murder of African "Americans" seeking safe haven with the British in an attempt to escape slavery during the U.S.-British War of 1812. This war was initiated with an act of aggression by the U.S. in its attempt to seize Canada from the British Empire. Seeing the U.S. flag survive a British bombardment in a battle for Fort McHenry, Francis Scott Key, the

slave owner and slavery advocate, was patriotically inspired to pen these commonly *unknown* lyrics/verses supporting U.S. slavery in "The Star-Spangled Banner":

No refuge could save the hireling and slave/From the terror of flight or the gloom of the grave/And the star-spangled banner in triumph doth wave/O'er the land of the free and the home of the brave.

Kaepernick's conscious protest would immediately categorize him with legendary Black athletes of principle like Jackie Robinson, Curt Flood, Muhammad Ali, Kareem Abdul-Jabbar, Tommie Smith and John Carlos who challenged the racial *politricks* of the country and the world, and would courageously manage the consequences.

Smith and Carlos' experiences with the FBI and their 1970s special Counter Intelligence Program (COINTELPRO) surveillance practices exemplify such consequences. Smith requested his FBI file under the Freedom of Information Act and was to find that he had "spent a long time on their top-10 list of subversive characters in the athletic world." Carlos also has a remembrance of politely drinking coffee in an agent's car outside of his home.

But like the societal and governmental hate and surveillance that ostensibly cost Tommie the life of his *Mulla* and his first marriage, John's family would not avoid the tragedy of loss. He concedes regrets for his shortcomings and failures of responsibility, financial and otherwise, in the loss of affection in his marriage. However, John also reveals the FBI's chicanery in sending his wife photos of John posing with random women, many college sorority students to whom he and Tommie would make speeches to earn scarce honorarium money. John states, "It got to the point where she was so paranoid, every time I went out the door...This started the very unraveling of my family."

Add financial woe, death threats and the bombardment of negative media scrutiny and one can witness a formula for depression with all of its symptoms of despair. Tommie remembers:

> I had to live in fear…every time I went home, hoping my house wouldn't be blown up or the windows shot up while my wife and son were inside. I would get knocks on the door and nobody would be there, or there would be a rap on the window or a phone call with no one at the other end, or someone shouting from the street. I wouldn't tell Denise, because she had enough on her mind, but I would quietly get up and take a walk outside to check.

Unemployed and depending on his wife's secretary salary, the Carlos family shattered by 1973 and was reduced to eating oatmeal at times for dinner. One evening, John would come home to a house emptied of his furniture and his family. His wife, Kim, had become worn-out and even in an unstable state, she decided to try her lot by herself with their two children. But in four years the dark clouds would consume Kim and in 1977 she would tragically take her own life, another horrible victim for Tommie and John's families from their 1968 protest.

Chapter Twelve

REDEMPTION: THERE IS NO FINISH LINE...

Despite the many years of hardships and tragedies after their Mexico City awards stand salute, Tommie and John's endurance would prevail to receive vindication. Today the world's social acceptance and present inspiration from their Black expression of power from the podium, more than 50 years ago, is their exaltation. Unfortunately, the accolades they receive today stem from the languishing conditions of White supremacy that still require the salute in protest. Although they shine today in the light of admiration as two most courageous men, years of humiliating obscurity were overcome to reach the present.

Tommie spent years at Oberlin College in Ohio away from the radar of surveillance, he thought. The hate mail and death threat phone calls would stop when he took a coaching job at Oberlin. The school had the right social history as a legendary stop for Black runaways escaping from American slavery. Oberlin is also the first college to admit women and African Americans.

Tommie coached, taught physical education classes, and became assistant, and eventually the athletic director at Oberlin. He brought his son Kevin to rear there, and met another woman named Denise who he married in 1976. Tommie would also pursue his master's degree, commuting to Cambridge College of Massachusetts to receive degrees in sociology and physical education. However, while trying to live low key at Oberlin, he was tracked and even formally interviewed by the FBI. Shortly after their visit, Tommie would be denied tenure at Oberlin and by the summer of 1978 he was again packing up and looking for work.

After sending out hundreds of resumes he finally received interest from Santa Monica College, a two year community college back in California. At Santa Monica he continued coaching and teaching sociology, again rising to become Athletic Director and raising a growing family as Denise would birth four children: Danielle, Anthony Kyle, Timothy and Joseph. After 24 years, however, their marriage ended.

Coming from such a large one himself, Tommie would always yearn for the comfort of family. He would meet and marry his third wife, Delois shortly after his divorce. In addition to taking care of his own five from the two Denises, he would also inherit Delois' children as a surrogate father.

Before eventually retiring from Santa Monica in 2005, Tommie would coach several Olympians including Johnny Gray, former American record holder for 800 meters. Upon retirement he moved to his wife's home state of Georgia. Although death threats and hate mail persist as commonplace in America, Tommie's message from the award stand has also persisted in Black athletic protests as well as through his wife's Delo2k Enterprises, Tommie Smith's marketing agency.

For John, the real race has also been one of endurance. With the responsibilities of single-parenthood added on his shoulders, John had to overcome his own depression and grab life's bucking bull by its horns and steady its course. Seen while doing landscaping to earn dollars, former football star Rosie Grier connected John with Los Angeles' first Black mayor, Tom Bradley. Bradley had been inspired by the 1968 Olympic protest, and arranged for Carlos to

become a community liaison through the Los Angeles City Council. He would transition this work into the creation of the John Carlos Youth Development League.

In 1984 with the Olympics arriving in Los Angeles, John wrote the Los Angeles Olympic Committee chair, San Jose State alumni Peter Ueberroth, requesting support for his youth league. Instead, Carlos was offered a position with the Olympic Committee; it was an opportunity to engage with the track and Olympic world, once again, on his own terms. The Olympic Committee job involved Carlos facilitating youth programs with the games. But perhaps the biggest surprise the job offered was the honor to run with the famed, flamed Olympic torch on its journey to the Los Angeles Coliseum. Tommie would receive the honor at Atlanta's 1996 games.

When the Los Angeles Olympics ended, so did the energy around Carlos' youth league. He would fold up his sleeves and start working again: any work, from aluminum mills to grocery stores. In life's shuffle, he would meet his present wife, Charlene, and join their families. John and Charlene, following his children's pleas, moved their new family out of Los Angeles and to the California desert community of Palm Springs. Carlos would eventually retire as a guidance counselor from Palm Springs High School. Getting to Palm Springs was John's way of going under the radar.

However, 2005 would mark Tommie and John's year of historical resurrection and redemption from where their ideas of protest were first kindled at San Jose State. Here, where fate would bring the two young men to be part of "Speed City," they would become part of so much more: the Human Rights Movement. A statue in honor of the Black salute had been commissioned and built at the center of the San Jose State University (SJSU) campus. In 2005, students at SJSU, who learned that Smith and Carlos were alumni, were challenged by Professor Cobie Harris to honor the largely ignored contribution of the two former student-athletes.

SJSU students raised $350,000 to have the statue built by sculptor Ricardo Gouveia, also known as Rigo 23. It is a magnificent twenty-five foot bronze, ceramic and fiberglass colossal perfectly resembling all the majestic courage and pride exhibited by Smith and Carlos on the victory stand that evening, October 16, 1968. Their black-gloved fists are heavens raised, heads bowed, with all of their symbolic adornments: black socks, beads, scarf, OPHR badges, and covered jersey.

An open place on the second-place stand beckons for visitors to join the struggle in the spirit of Australian silver medalist Peter Norman. The victory stand in 1968 would birth a brotherhood between the three men, brothers from different mothers, but from the same Master's plan. Norman would speak at the statue's unveiling ceremony in 2005; Smith and Carlos would honorably serve as pallbearers the following year when Peter Norman sadly transitioned from a heart attack and joined The Ancestors of the struggle for human equality.

Also present at Smith and Carlos' honoring were the erudite OPHR founder and UCLA-Berkley Sociology professor emeritus Dr. Harry Edwards, as well as fellow OPHR member, SJSC alumni, 1968 Olympic champion and former world record holder, Lee Evans. Carlos would correctly acknowledge that Evans deserved to have a statue in his honor as well. Evans, like the others, would receive the death threats for his OPHR involvement. He would continue running after the Olympics and retired in 1980 at the age of thirty-three, posting a time of 46.5 that final year. Evans went on to head national athletic programs in six African countries as well as work as head coach at the University of South Alabama.

Dr. Edwards has gone on to continue to encourage stronger Black management participation in professional sports, serving as a consultant for the Golden State Warriors basketball team, the San Francisco 49ers football team, and all three major sports leagues. Is it a small irony that Colin Kaepernick played for the same 49ers that

Edwards consults? Kaepernick in 2016, undoubtedly influenced by Smith and Carlos' 1968 national anthem protest, sent the American sports world into confusion when he sat for, and eventually took a knee to the playing of the U.S. national anthem in protest to the U.S. criminal court system's unaccountability for police killings of unarmed Black people.

Eric Read and Eli Howard would be among his teammates and others in the NFL who would join Kaepernick in protest. Eventually dismissed from the 49ers, Kaepernick would be *"white-balled"* from any further job opportunities in the NFL. However, Kaepernick's sacrifice has caused a great awakening in a wave of modern-day Black athletes who are recognizing their potential as active agents in society beyond the field and court. Kaepernick would eventually withdraw his legal grievance filed against the NFL for colluding to keep him out of the league, after the NFL settled for an undisclosed confidential amount.

The year 2016 would also mark Smith and Carlos' official reconciliation with the IOC and American society. President Barack Obama honored the two men at a White House ceremony as they were named Olympic ambassadors. President Obama would acknowledge that truth bearers in society have often not had their messages comprehended until years later. Clearly this is the case with the *power from the podium* expressed by Smith and Carlos on October 16, 1968. And the power of their protest endures in today's generation of athletes.

In 2020, NBA players were compelled to use the power of the *mancott* to express their disdain and protest the continual onslaught against Black people's lives in the present world. Five minutes before their August 26, 2020 basketball game, the Milwaukee Bucs players decided they would not play ball while protests ensued in the aftermath of the Kenosha, Wisconsin police shooting of the African American father, Jacob Blake. At point blank range, Blake was shot seven times in his back in front of his three sons! Blake survived the

shots, by the grace of The Almighty, paralyzed from a severed spinal cord with internal organ damage.

Regardless of the racial slur of slavery subtly associated with the team's name, and cultural slurs of many other American sports franchises, the Bucs *mancott* decision would influence the postponement of the NBA playoffs. Their *mancott* would also exhibit, if only symbolically, the potential of Black athletes to altogether shut down American sports industries in protest to the apparent genocide being leveled against Black and Brown people worldwide. Unfortunately, the world still requires the present demands of a Black Lives Matter movement. Eternal gratitude from the *downpressed* will forever enshrine those in the world of sports who sacrifice their love for sport for a greater love for humanity to protest against the people's persecution and victimization in the new world *disorder*. Of genocide, in his last book, *Where Do We Go From Here: Chaos or Community*, Dr. King wrote:

> Since racism is based on the dogma 'that the hope of civilization depends upon eliminating some races and keeping others pure,' its ultimate logic is genocide…While America has not literally sought to eliminate the Negro in this final sense, it has, through the system of segregation, substituted a subtle reduction of life by means of deprivation.

King's words put all of humanity in the moral crossroads regarding the explosive topic of racism. Hence, any modern-day athlete who seeks to express their cultural-political voice on behalf of the people, in the midst of this world of calamity, will be in some way connected to the spirit for justice elevated to the heavens in the black-gloved fists of Tommie Smith and John Carlos, and their triumphant expression of *Power from the Podium*.

A luta continua. The struggle continues.

ACKNOWLEDGEMENTS

F orever giving thanks and praises to The Highest, Head Creator, *Omniversal* Almighty. Forever giving thanks and praises for the Angelic Powers and Ancestors that have all aligned my life's journey with this most blessed path that I have been given to travel.

Track and Field is a sport that was part of my family tradition from the time my grandfather was a youth growing up in Harlem in the 1920s. My father carried it on in the 1950s and his high school gold, silver and bronze medals displayed in our home would, many a youthful day, fascinate my mind as I would try to imagine him running the races that won him the awards; I even recall my mom having a medal in the display.

However, the most compelling track and field memento that would captivate my attention in our home was a framed poster of the gold and bronze medal winners of the 1968 Olympics 200-meter dash. Tommie Smith and John Carlos are not running in arguably the most reproduced image of the Mexico City games. In the poster, the two young men give the Black Power Salute in protest of the injustice and atrocities plaguing the Black American condition of their times. Growing up with that icon in my room would profoundly influence a courage and desire to live, in some way, as part of the struggle to advance my people's cultural-political power as an ascendant of African ancestry in the Western hemisphere. The Black Power Salute, for as long as I can remember, was me and my brother's favorite picture-taking pose, and a special connection I felt with the bronze medal winner when I learned that my mother (Dawn Burrowes Patterson) was John Carlos' classmate when she arrived from Kingston, Jamaica and attended middle school in Harlem.

I went to college on track scholarships and re-united a few summers ago with my high school and college teammate and friend, Mark Taylor, who now lives in San Jose, California. Visiting him for the first time in 20 years, I encouraged him to bring his young family to a monument that was built on the campus of San Jose State University in honor of Tommie Smith and John Carlos, 1968 alumni of the school. Seeing and posing with the monument I remembered, with goosebumps, youthful days in my room staring and reflecting on the courage of these two young men to take their pinnacle moment of athletic accomplishment and fame and livicate (dedicate) it in protest for their colonized people against their birth country's denial of their people's equal human rights. After posing at the monument with my friend and his daughters, Jasmine and Naomi, we visited the campus library to fulfill the desire of his young, precocious, and avid readers. Serving the broader city community, the college library had its own children's section.

With the librarian's help we searched, without success, for a children's book telling the story behind the scholar-athlete-activists' statute positioned in the center of the campus. It was Jasmine's unfulfilled desire to read about the men in the monument that sparked my desire to research and write this book on the lives of Olympians Tommie Smith and John Carlos, from their childhoods to their experiences on their return to the U.S. after their most famous/infamous 1968 Olympic medal stand protest.

Although paling by comparison, my own track and field experiences, inspired in part by Smith and Carlos, without doubt, were essential to this book's creation. The two men's race of expertise would become, in a way, my own as I was an NCAA All-Conference Athlete in the same 200 meters. I was an aficionado-participant from age eight to twenty-two, and still, all operations cease when a track meet is on television.

In addition to acknowledging with the deepest gratitude my born, immediate and extended family for sharing and supporting in the cultivation of this book, there are many others to acknowledge for helping to shape the track and sports love and discipline that have been central to all of my life achievements: The Greenburgh Parkway Gardens Youth Massive, (1974–1984), Uncle/Godfather/Coach Charles Poussaint, Coach Robert (Bob) Smith, RIP, (and all the members of the great Jaguar Track Club NYC), Coach Brian Denman (and the members of the great 1976–77, 1979 NYC U.S. Youth Games Track Teams), Coach John "Speedy" Alston (and the members of the 1980 Kenyan Runners, Brooklyn, NY), Coach James Farley (Fairview-Greenburgh, NY Striders), Coach Ken Kotler (Woodlands HS), Coach Carol Ann Coram (Woodlands HS), Coach John Miller (Woodlands HS), Woodlands High School Track Teammates (1980-84), Coach William P. Moultrie, RIP, (and the members of the great Howard University Track Team 1984-85), Coach Diana Valdez (Valdez Striders), Coach Charlie Strong (and the members of the University of South Carolina Track Team 1985-88), football coaches (Doug Plath/Hartsdale Dad's Club, John House/Woodlands HS, Larry Warren/Woodlands HS, Chris Pinto/Woodlands HS).

Giving thanks for my Africana Studies Temple University graduate school professors, colleagues and experiences that give me confidence to write and participate in the restoration of our culture and heritage.

Giving thanks for Nassau Community College supporting the sabbatical leave to research and write the initial manuscript/draft for this book.

Giving thanks for my son, Jahlil Shabazz, who inspired the book's title; giving thanks for the many who have read parts, or the whole of this manuscript and have given *feedblack*, shared testimonies and/or connections, including: Dr. Sonia Peterson-Lewis, DJ Duane Hume, Baba Jerry Glanville, Professor Patrick Payne, Dr. Kofi Barima, Dr. Ella Forbes, Dr. James Conyers, Dr. Brandon M. Stanford, Coach JAM Shakwi, Coach George Cherry, and Coach Ron Johnson.

Giving thanks for my *heartist*, Kephera Ife, for putting her soul into the artwork for this project.

Giving thanks for Patrice Samara and the Wordeee team for all the professional and technical assistance in helping to manifest this project to the fullness.

Finally, giving thanks for this generation's youth that inspire me, including: Nesta, Naiyirah, Nima, Salim, Tsahai, Tseday, Salahedin, Elias, Layla, Sara, Semirah, Amare, Jasmine, Naomi, The Learning Tree scholars, and the NRG Track Club runners, among others. Prayerfully, you all receive the inspired call in your hearts to embrace and represent the best of yourselves in connection to our heritage and, in your own way, express your *Power From the Podium* for generations to come.

ABOUT THE AUTHOR

R.A. Ptahsen-Shabazz, Ph.D.

R.A. Ptahsen-Shabazz, Ph.D. is a Black/ Africana Studies educator as professor of Africana Studies at Nassau Community College in Long Island, NY. Born and raised between the Bronx and Westches- ter, Dr. Ptahsen-Shabazz is of Jamaican maternal and African-American paternal heritage. He attended college on track scholarships received from Howard University and the University of South Carolina, the latter where he graduated with a Bachelor of Arts degree in Broadcast Journalism and Mass Communications. He then attended graduate school at Temple University earning Master of Arts and Ph.D. degrees in African American Studies. Dr. Ptahsen-Shabazz has committed his life to researching and teaching on the often-forgotten contributions that Black/African people have made to human culture and progress; on such topics he has spoken internationally. Dr. Ptahsen-Shabazz' premier book was *Black to the Roots: Reggae's Rise, Downpression and Reascension.*

ABOUT THE "HEARTIST"

Kephera Ife

Born on the island of Jamaica and immigrating to the United States at the age of twelve, Kephera Ife showed early signs of being an artist/clothing designer. She graduated from Syracuse University with a BA in Fashion Design in 1998. Turning her main focus to art, she started with fashion illustrations and eventually ventured into realism. Keeping her original stylized signature drawing style, it evolved over time into a mix of pop culture and the cultural experience of growing up in the African diaspora, adding sculptures to the mix in 2020. She hopes for her art to keep growing and reach more people. "Art should never be complicated. Bind your soul to it and you will reach the minds and hearts of others for eternity."

www.ingramcontent.com/pod-product-compliance
Lightning Source LLC
Chambersburg PA
CBHW051634120626
46551CB00014B/2069